MW01043421

Guys, Are We Really Listening?

How to Become a More Effective Listener

Howard Binkow

Copyright 2002 by Howard Binkow. All rights reserved. No part of this book may be reproduced, stored in retrieval systems, or transmitted in any form, by any means, including mechanical, electronic, photocopying, recording or otherwise, without prior written permission of the publisher.

ISBN: 0-9715390-0-6
SAN # 254 8119
Library of Congress Control Number 2001130497

Thunderbolt Publishing
1355 W. Palmetto Park Rd. #210
Boca Raton, Florida, 33486
WeDoListen.com

Printed in the United States of America

10 9 8 7 6 5 4 3 2 1

*This book is dedicated to any man honest
and courageous enough to recognize
he needs a little help in order
to become a more effective listener.*

Acknowledgments

I wrote this book; the extraordinary women in my life explained it to me.

Listen to the essence of things.

—Heraclitus

Disclaimer

The purpose of this book is to educate, entertain, and share the passion I have for the art of understanding what is being communicated.

I encourage you to learn more about listening from this source and others and to tailor the information to meet your individual needs and situation. Use good judgment and if your therapist, family members, or friends disagree with something I have written, please listen to them.

Howard Binkow, Author

Contents

The world is not to be narrowed
till it will go into the understanding...
but the understanding is to be expanded
till it can take in the world.

—Francis Bacon

Introduction

When people talk, listen completely.
Most people never listen.

—Ernest Hemingway

I thought I was a good listener and I was not. Improving my listening skills has led me to have everything I need in life including more than enough money, better relationships and great sex.

My purpose in writing this book is to share with as many men as possible what it takes to become a more effective listener. And for future generations, my goal is to persuade our public school systems to offer courses in listening.

The only prerequisite to being a more effective listener is a genuine interest in understanding another person's point of view, needs, and feelings. Without that intent, this book will be a waste of time.

With the help of friends, family, authors, and teachers, I have attempted to condense in simple language what women instinctively know about listening and what little boys ought to have been taught in grade school. Any profits from the sale of this book will be used to help create a course in listening for our public school systems.

With the possibility of improving your life and the lives of those around you, consider investing some of your valuable time to learn more about the art of understanding what is being communicated. You will then understand what it means to listen more effectively. At the very least, you will know when you are not listening. I know it will take time, but can you imagine what the world would be like if more of us guys were really listening?

If you would like instant gratification without reading further, cut out, and give away the **Gold Listening Cards** that are found at the back of the book.

During listening opportunities that involve both thoughts and feelings of important people in your life, do the best you can to listen in the way suggested on the card. If you read the rest of this book, you will learn how to consistently deliver what the card promises.

A friend who is gender correct felt that using the word "girlfriend" throughout the book was not appropriate for an adult. Aside from the fact that my adult status is questionable, my intent is not to offend anyone. My girlfriend, who happens to be a lady, told me that she was quite happy being referred to as a girlfriend, for now.

I apologize for any sweeping generalizations, strong opinions, or prejudices. They are offered because this is my book.

PART 1

A Listening Success Story

Wisdom is the reward for a lifetime of listening
when you'd rather be talking.

—Aristotle

My two ex-wives pleaded with me to "just listen." I had no idea what they were talking about. Since they didn't offer listening courses in the schools I attended, I made up my own listening standards. In my infinite wisdom, I decided that being semi-quiet when someone was speaking made me an excellent listener.

I thought listening meant to hear some of the words while I was preparing to speak. I made little eye contact with the speaker and paid no attention to his or her non- verbal messages. And, on a regular basis, I interrupted to offer unsolicited advice or solutions. I was completely unaware of my listening "blind spots."

PART 1

Changing my Perspective

In 1990, I listened to an audiotape by Stephen Covey titled, *First Seek to Understand Before Being Understood*. It acted as a wake up call for me. I had not considered that notion before. Since I grow by recognizing my imperfections, I began an obsessive-compulsive journey to listen in a different way.

I read every book on the subject of listening I could find and joined the International Listening Association. When I was packing to go to the ILA annual convention in Chicago a friend asked, "Who will be speaking?"

After learning how successful author-teachers describe listening, I re-rated my listening ability from excellent to below average. I then made a personal commitment to listen with the goal to understand, not with the intent to talk.

At Work

Work was an easy place to try out my new listening skills. Nine years ago at the age of sixty, I found myself out of work and out of money. Being old and poor is not a good combination. It had taken me twenty years as a homebuilder to become a millionaire and another twenty years to spend it all. And, I had a ball doing both.

At a time when most men are thinking about retirement and with no previous experience in sales, I started a career as a traveling salesman selling automobile extended warranty programs to credit unions. Credit union executives get dozens of calls every week from vendors trying to sell them something. Most do not get an appointment. Instead of trying to sell over the phone, I requested a meeting to listen and learn about the credit union to determine whether our program would be of benefit to their members.

I always got an appointment and started selling only after listening and understanding the needs of the credit union and then tailoring my proposal to meet those needs. Fortunately, as of this date, the competition is not using this same approach.

In the sales training sessions I conduct for the company I represent, I ask new salespeople, "What is the most important element of a sale?" No one, young or old, has ever responded, "Meeting customer needs." You can't meet someone's needs if you haven't taken the time to listen and understand what they are.

As a result of my "listen and understand first" sales strategy along with a little luck and timing, I sold my program to several of the largest credit unions in the country. Within two years, my yearly income was in the middle six figures and I have maintained that level ever since. I now work an average of ten hours a week and value my work time at one thousand dollars per hour. Ninety percent of my time is spent listening and understanding, and ten percent talking and taking action.

Although I now recognize the value of listening effectively and have reaped the benefits of doing so, it was not always that way. In my first career out of college I became a partner in one of the country's largest home building companies and bossed lots of people around. I formed opinions, made decisions, and influenced others without making a serious attempt to understand the needs of our customers. It helped that we were in a seller's market. I designed and built thousands of houses for low- to moderate-income people with living rooms facing the rear.

Late in my career I saw a photograph by San Francisco photographer Bill Owens showing a husband, wife, and little boy sitting on beach chairs in their driveway in front of an open garage door. The caption said, "Our house is built with the living room in the back so in the evenings we sit out front..." It never occurred to me that many families preferred the social benefits of a living room facing the street. What a difference in the quality and comfort of their lives I could have made if I had been available to listen!

In Relationships

There were also immediate benefits in my personal life. My newly found listening ability helped me communicate better with women, the rest of my family, and the challenging people at work.

Looking back, I'm afraid I was not very successful at getting along better with women by trying to figure them out; although I had spent a great deal of time and effort trying to do so. I did discover something important while pursuing this impossible task: women have inherent listening skills that men do not. It has to do in part with a woman's nurturing nature and the fact that her eyes can see in three hundred sixty degrees and that she can do more than one thing at a time.

When we are out for dinner, my girlfriend can have an intense conversation with me, observe what the couple at the next table is having for dinner, and listen to another conversation across the room. On my best day I can't do that.

A woman's nurturing role makes it much easier for her to listen and understand the message behind the message. I had convinced myself that I could not do this and "read between the lines." It was a made-up story because with practice, I *am* able do it.

Even though I do not yet completely understand women, my life is much easier and happier when my girlfriend, daughter, and sister sense that I am listening and *trying* to understand them. Listening to and acknowledging these three women is a continuous process because their moods and desires change and so yesterday's understanding may no longer apply.

PART 1

My experience is that once you learn how to listen effectively to a woman, listening to the rest of the family and the rest of the world will be a snap.

Great Sex

A wise investment of time is the fifteen to thirty minutes a day I spend listening to and acknowledging my loving girlfriend without interrupting or offering unsolicited advice and solutions. If this simple act of acknowledgment happens to take place before we make love, it become fabulous foreplay and is the ultimate aphrodisiac.

Communication...

is the key element of a healthy relationship.

R. Hicinbothem

PART II

How Effective a Listener are You Now?

*The deepest need of the human
soul is to be understood, affirmed,
validated, and appreciated.*

—Stephen Covey

It has been said that the real art of conversation is to say the right thing at the right time and also leave unsaid the wrong thing at a tempting moment. Before you take on this challenging task, invest two or three minutes of your valuable time to complete the following listening evaluation that is based upon listening skills taught by self-help gurus like Stephen Covey and John Gray.

On a scale of one to ten, with ten being the highest level, rate yourself as to how well you listen on a consistent basis to your mate, parents,

9

children, siblings, and the challenging people at work.

While listening,

_____ 1. I suspend judgment and have a genuine desire to understand another person's point of view, needs, and feelings.

_____ 2. I am a patient, accepting, and thoughtful listener.

_____ 3. I avoid distractions, give my undivided attention, and remember what has been said.

_____ 4. I acknowledge the speaker's feelings, and rarely interrupt or offer unsolicited advice and solutions.

_____ 5. I listen with the goal to understand what is being communicated, not with the intent to talk.

_____ 6. I am in constant eye contact with the speaker and am interested in what is being said.

How Effective a Listener are You Now?

_____ 7. I observe non-verbal messages and can "read between the lines."

_____ 8. I positively reinforce the speaker in a way that invites the conversation to continue.

_____ 9. I stay calm and cool when the speaker is angry or upset.

_____ 10. I listen to my full potential. Before forming an opinion or taking action, I keep an open mind and understand the entire message to the satisfaction of the speaker.

_____ 11. I listen to others as I would have others listen to me.

_____   TOTAL RESULTS

If you are a man and scored above zero, there is a high probability that you have considerably overestimated your listening skills.

If your total was 110, congratulations on being a perfect listener. I assume that on a regular basis you receive compliments on your listening ability from your wife or girlfriend and the rest of your family.

Other scores:

61-109:   Above average listener
40- 60:   Average listener
0 – 39:   You have some serious work to do

Are you ready to admit that you have room for improvement in such an important skill as listening? And are you open to the possibility that the quality of your life and the lives of those around you will dramatically improve if you become a more effective listener? Are you willing to do something about it?

If the answer to each of these questions is "yes," you are well along the path to becoming a more effective listener.

Retain your scores and re-rate yourself after thirty days of listening more effectively.

...I also think listening is as important as talking. It's interesting; if you're a good listener, people often compliment you for being a good conversationalist.

—Jesse Ventura

PART III

Anticipate the Benefits

*All speech, written or spoken,
is a dead language until it finds
a willing and prepared listener.*

—Robert Louis Stevenson

Once you become a more effective listener, you will find it easier to get along with the woman in your life, the rest of your family including teenagers, and the challenging people at work. And, you will have uncovered a way to improve your sex life (excuse the pun) and how to make money and work less.

Who would you rather spend time with, someone who talks too much or someone who listens well?

Listening with the goal to understand is an active, inspired, and compassionate act that will create an atmosphere of trust with everyone in your life. Being heard makes a person feel that he or

15

she counts and that you care. It is not necessary that you agree or completely understand. If you make an honest effort to understand, the person will appreciate it so much that he or she will search for ways to make your life easier and happier. Give more effective listening a try; you will be pleased with the results.

Get Along Better with the Woman in Your Life

According to Warren Farrell, marriage counselor, *I've never heard a wife say, 'I want a divorce, my husband understands me.'* There are men who say that women nag and complain too much. Women would not nag and complain so much if they felt they were being heard.

How many painful discussions have there been when you have been accused of not listening and you think you have been listening? Women love it when men pay attention and listen without interrupting or giving unsolicited advice and solutions. Consider making yourself available to listen to your wife or girlfriend for up to one hour every night. Listen to her with the same respect and interest as you would your boss or best customer. If you listen well enough so that she feels appreciated, acknowledged, and understood, the quality of both your lives will dramatically improve.

While listening, give your undivided attention and keep quiet except to acknowledge that you are awake and interested. In exchange for you providing this quality listening time, chances improve that your partner will give you more joy than you ever imagined. If your significant other is qualifying for the talking Olympics, you have my sympathy. Set a time limit for listening, think about her other qualities, and move on.

Improve Your Sex Life

Has your partner ever been less than amorous after mentioning that you are not listening and paying attention to her? My experience is that you can improve the quality and quantity of your sex life by first having the patience to take time to listen to and acknowledge the thoughts and feelings of your partner.

For a woman, feeling like she is being heard and validated before lovemaking is a most erotic form of foreplay. When she feels this way, sex will become more intense, rewarding, longer lasting, and more fun for both of you. Some ideas on how to help make a woman feel that way are covered later in this book.

Make More Money and Work Less

Are you working hard and not making as much money as you feel you are entitled? If you want to make more money and work less, listen more and talk less. You will then be able to learn more about the needs of customers, clients, the competition, partners, bosses, employees, and co-workers. And, listening with the goal to understand will save you lots of time by not having to repeat the same tasks.

Bond with Your Teenager

And you thought it couldn't be done! Being a more effective listener works especially well with teenagers, even with those teens who know everything and/or have perfected the art of selective listening.

Persistence, not insistence, is the key to persuasion. You cannot persuade a teenager by insisting that he or she see things your way. You can persist until you see things his or her way and begin to understand the message behind the words.

You can learn more about what a wonderful person your child really is through listening. Be available to listen effectively when a teen wants to talk and you will find that he or she might want to communicate with you more often.

Understanding a teenager does not mean you have to agree or relinquish your right to ask a teen to take responsibility for his or her actions.

PART IV

The Path of More Effective Listening

*If you don't know where you are going,
you might not get there.*

—Yogi Berra

Step 1:
Have the Desire, Make a Commitment

The only pre-requisite to becoming a more effective listener is the desire to understand another person's point of view, needs, and feelings. You cannot, however, fake desire because whatever you are thinking, you are doing, and that is what the speaker is feeling. Energy follows thought, intention, and action.

PART IV

Having the Desire...or Not

David Barkan wrote, *Easy listening occurs only on the radio*. A friend is a sales representative for a five-star hotel in Europe. Her job requires she listen carefully in order to understand the needs of her clients. She has trouble listening to her mother and sister because "they ramble on and what they have to say is not very interesting." My friend has the ability but not the desire to listen and understand her mother and sister.

Make a commitment to become a more effective listener. What Winston Churchill had to say still holds true, *Courage is what it takes to stand up and speak; courage is also what it takes to sit down and listen.*

My best friend and his son love each other and go through bouts of not liking one another. The son's actions clearly indicate that he is not committed to understanding his father's points of view, needs, or feelings. When the father expresses them, the son tunes out and refuses to listen. The result is that both are stuck in an unhealthy, unfulfilling relationship.

As with everything of value, more effective listening takes work and is worth while. During times you are already listening, change your listening routine.

✖ For at least fifteen minutes a day, take advantage of important listening opportunities that involve thoughts and feelings of those you interact with at home, work, or play. If you invest more than fifteen minutes a day, you will receive the benefits faster. If you miss one day, increase the time to thirty minutes the following day.

✗ Offer **Gold Listening Cards** as seen below. For your daily homework, cut out and give away the **Cards** (supplied on the last page of this book) to people at home, work, or play. Do the best you can to live up to what is promised on the **Card**.

An easy way to get started is to give the cards to people at work. You will be amazed at how much they will open up.

Gold Listening Card

This card entitles bearer to 15 minutes of my face-to-face undivided attention. I commit to listen with the goal to understand what is being communicated, not with the intent to talk. I agree to acknowledge feelings and promise not to interrupt or offer unsolicited advice and solutions.
I will listen in the same way, as I would have others listen to me.

Signed_____

www.WeDoListen.com

When you give Gold Listening Cards to a spouse or family member, explain that you are learning how to be a more effective listener and ask for their help and patience.

PART IV

Ask the speakers to grade you on a scale of one to ten, with ten being the most effective, as to how well you listened as described on the card.

Recycle the cards and re-use them as often as you can. When you listen as promised you will be opening up a listening bank account with the speaker. When more deposits than withdrawals are made, you will begin to receive the dividends.

You are what your deep driving desire is;
as your desire is so is your will;
as your will is so is your deed;
as your deed is so is your destiny.

—The Upanishads

Step 2:
Accept the Challenges
and Recognize the Opportunities

It is the disease of not listening, the malady of not marking that I am troubled with.

—William Shakespeare

Those of us who want to become more effective listeners must overcome several challenges.

✗ No clear standards of listening excellence exist.

✗ Old listening habits and patterns are often difficult to change.

✖ Men and women have different opinions of what it means to "really listen."

By avoiding selective listening and learning to listen objectively you can convert the challenges into opportunities.

The Challenges

I wish I had known earlier in life that there was more to listening than being quiet.

✖ No clear standards of listening excellence exist due in part to the public school systems not offering courses in listening.

Were you ever taught the difference between hearing and listening? The "can you hear me?" that we constantly say on our cell phones is not the same as "are you listening to me?" Even the several dictionaries I read offered no clear, agreed-upon definition of "to hear" and "to listen."

For the purposes of more effective listening; "to hear" is to *accurately receive and send sounds to the brain;* "to listen" is **the art of understanding what is being communicated**. A big difference, isn't there?

✖ Old listening habits and patterns are hard to change. Author and educator Huston Smith told me, *I visited a nun whom I hadn't seen in several years and when I asked her what was new, she said, 'I*

23

PART IV

have a new mantra which I say several
times a day; maybe I'm wrong.'

If you want to listen effectively you are going to have to be willing to acquire some new habits and change some old ones. We often cannot prevent slipping into old habits and patterns because we are in them before we have a chance to think. Awareness is the key. If you become aware that you are stuck in an old habit you want to get rid of, you can then do something about it.

To reinforce this idea, I will share a story that has been circulating the Internet. A new monk arrives at a monastery and is assigned to help the other monks in copying the old texts by hand. He notices, however, that they are copying from copies, not the original manuscripts. The new monk asks the head monk about this; pointing out that if there were an error in the first copy, that error would be continued in all of the subsequent copies. The head monk replies, "We have been copying from the copies for centuries, but you make a good point, my son." The head monk goes down to the cellar with one of the copies to check it out against the original.

Hours go by without anyone seeing the head monk. One of the monks goes to the cellar to look for him. He hears sobbing coming from the back of the cellar and finds the old monk leaning over on the original books crying. He asks the head monk what's wrong, and in a choked voice came the reply, "The word is celebrate."

The Path of More Effective Listening

✗ Men and women have different opinions of what it means to "really listen."

John Gray writes, *Once upon a time Martians and Venusians met, fell in love, and had happy relationships together because they respected and accepted their differences. They then came to earth and amnesia set in. They forgot they were from different planets.*

When it comes to listening, women are genetically superior. Women intuitively know how to listen whereas men mistakenly think they know how to listen. I don't like breaking male ranks but the simple truth is that women, even when they are not listening, know more about effective listening than men do. I rate myself an excellent listener among men and slightly above average among my women friends. We men, however, can become more effective listeners because it is a learned skill.

In social situations when I mentioned that I was writing a book called *Guys, Are We Really Listening?* every woman applauded my honesty and offered to buy a copy. The men seemed uniformly disinterested in the subject with comments like, "Oh, that's interesting." When one of my friends suggested to her husband that he read this book, he responded in a not-so-loving tone; "*You* are the one who needs to learn how to listen." Guys, I guess we don't know what we don't know. If you think you know more about listening than the lady in your life, you might want to consider getting a second opinion.

If a man is alone and talking in the woods with no woman present to listen, is he still wrong? Here's an inclusive but not exclusive list of why women know more about effective listening.

Women

✖ are inherently empathic

✖ are people and relationship oriented

✖ notice and understand non-verbal clues

✖ ask more questions

✖ see the whole picture

✖ are skilled at multi-tasking

✖ listen for feelings and mood

✖ remember what is said

Men outshine women in

✖ overestimating their listening abilities

✖ hearing only the gist of a conversation

✖ having a short attention span

✖ interrupting

✖ controlling and suppressing feelings

✖ focusing on one thing at a time

✖ not taking advice, solutions, or directions

✖ giving advice, solutions, and directions

Opportunities

Avoid selective listening. As Dick Cavett said, *It takes a rare person to hear what he doesn't want to hear.* Typically, we listen to about twenty-five percent of our potential, which means we ignore, forget, or misunderstand seventy-five percent of what we hear. Selective listening is a choice. We tend to listen least when we need to listen most.

This happens when we are

✖ disinterested, distracted, lazy, or bored

✖ not willing to spend time listening

✖ hearing only what we want to hear

✖ taking the speaker for granted

✖ overlooking the real meaning when a speaker beats around the bush and codes his or her messages

✖ afraid something will come up that we may not be able to handle

✖ thinking our views might be overlooked, rejected or ridiculed

✖ believing we might have to change, risk losing control, compromise, or give in

✖ thinking that listening and understanding means agreement

PART IV

Listen Objectively

There is an art in listening. To be able to listen one must abandon or put aside all prejudices, pre-formulations, and daily activities. When you are in a receptive state of mind, things can be easily understood: you are listening when your real attention is given to something. But unfortunately we listen through a screen of resistance.

—Jiddu Krishnamurti

    Listening objectively means to set aside personal filters like judgments, beliefs, prejudices, or interpretations. Examples of personal filters might be pre-judging a person by his/her appearance, voice, thoughts, views, feelings, or intentions, or saying:

- ✖ "That doesn't make sense to me."
- ✖ "I'm right, you are wrong."
- ✖ "I'm bored."
- ✖ "I can't wait to hear what I did wrong."

Do you know any of the following listening types? (from *The 5 Keys To Power Listening* by Rochelle Devereaux)

PHONY LISTENER: appears to hear while his eyes roam around and his body turns away

GREEDY ORATOR: waits for a pause to speak

28

The Path of More Effective Listening

SCREENER: filters out what he does not want to hear

DODGER: avoids uncomfortable subjects; pretends that he is listening and then changes the subject

WORRIER: anticipates personal attacks and is defensive and does not listen to what you are saying

ENTRAPPER: finds a way to make you look bad

UNCONSCIOUS CONVERSER: only hears the words

KNOW-IT-ALL: talks to himself

OSTRICH: does not want to hear anything that may cause discomfort

FOG MACHINE: is wrapped up in his own words

KARATE MASTER: is alert to danger and when he hears intimidation, he strikes

JUMPER: leaps from one topic to another

TURTLE: plods along and can't keep up

HARE: rushes ahead

CHARCOAL FILTER: only hears what he likes

POLITE PRETENDER: graciously ignores speaker

THE INTERRUPTER: feels he would forget what he had to say if he didn't interrupt

THE SELF-CONSCIOUS LISTENER: wonders if he looks okay and if the speaker finds him smart

THE INTELLECTUAL OR LOGICAL LISTENER: hears only with his head; hears only what he wants to hear and blots out large areas of reality

PART IV

Exercise

Read one of the feature articles from a magazine like *TIME* or *Newsweek*. Think about your opinion of the article, the writer's point of view, the tone and the accuracy, or credibility of the named sources. Were the points well supported? Get the next issue of the same magazine and read the letters from readers. You will usually find points of view different from yours. Reread the article, keeping the other readers' comments in mind. It will be interesting to notice something you may have missed or interpreted differently. Whether you agree or disagree is not the point. What's important is to accept other people's observations as valid perceptions. (From *The Zen of Listening* by Rebecca Shafir)

Step 3:
Pay Attention

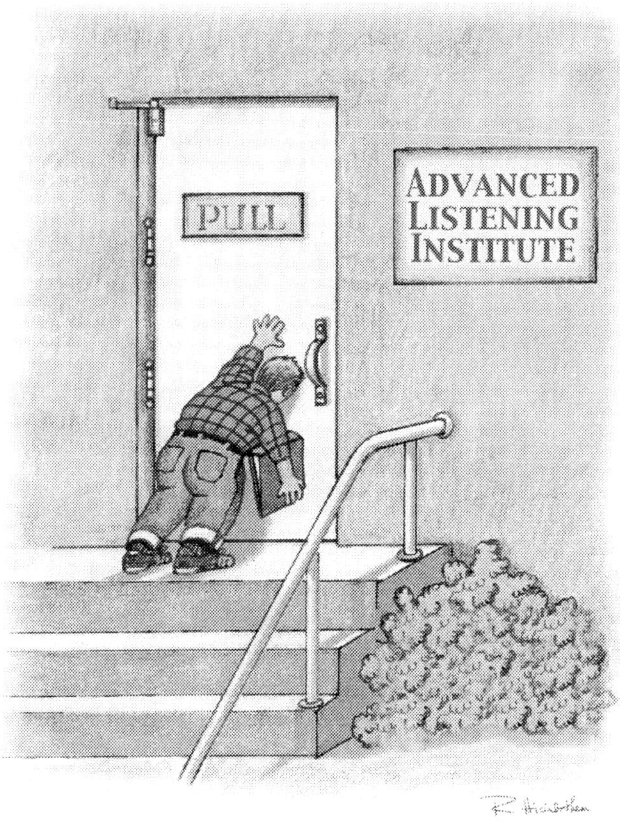
PULL
ADVANCED
LISTENING
INSTITUTE

PART IV

*I always know when I am conscious,
but for some strange reason, I never
know when I am unconscious.*

—Ashleigh Brilliant

On a Regular Basis, Are You Listening Attentively?

One day while I was editing this section of the book, a two-paragraph flyer was slipped under my apartment door. It was from the management of the high-rise building in which I live. The first paragraph announced that the following Monday they would be testing the building's fire alarm system. I read the first paragraph and did not pay attention to the second.

On Monday, as promised, the test sirens blasted into my apartment. I was on the phone when a voice came through the alarm system's speaker: "This is an emergency and not a test. There is an actual fire in the building. Please evacuate immediately. Use the stairways and not the elevators." The improbability of a fire occurring during a fire alarm test did not register in my mind.

The only item of clothing I was wearing at the time was a skimpy Speedo bathing suit my family begged me not to buy or wear in public, and a pair of flip-flops.

I took my wallet, money, and cell phone, and said goodbye to everything else I owned. It took me only a few minutes to flip-flop down ten floors to the lobby. I never imagined what I might look like on the TV evening news standing half naked next to the fire engines.

The man at the front desk looked too calm for someone who was in a burning building. With a sad, disappointed look on his face, he asked if I had read the entire flyer. In the second paragraph was written. "The audible part of the system will be tested, please ignore all commands as they pertain to testing only."

My embarrassing experience did drive home the point that being present and paying attention is a continuous process. If you snooze, you lose.

My girlfriend threatens to picket one of my book signings with a sign saying, "This man does not always pay attention and listen." Do the best you can and don't expect perfection because no one can pay attention and listen effectively all the time. It takes way too much energy. If you really want to learn how to pay attention, write a book on listening. It will remind you, as it does me, to practice what your preach.

Become Quiet in a Quiet Place

How many times have you come home from a hard day at work needing a little peace and quiet and your family wants your immediate attention?

If you are too tired, busy, or pressured to give your undivided attention, ask for a "time out" and agree upon another time to listen. When that time comes, find a quiet place conducive to listening with few or no distractions. Your being present, aware, interested, and available to listen will help make it a special moment for the speaker.

Give Your Undivided Attention

*You cannot truly listen to anyone
and do anything else at the same time.*

—M. Scott Peck.

It is easy to lose concentration while listening because our brains can process five hundred spoken words per minute while the average person speaks at a rate of one hundred fifty words per minute.

At one point in my life I convinced myself that I had too many things on my mind to give undivided attention. But I was kidding myself. I have always given my full attention when watching a good movie or when I thought a beautiful woman was beckoning me with her smile.

According to psychologist, Homer Hardaway, *You cannot change your destination overnight; you can change your direction overnight.* We all know how to pay attention when we consider something interesting or if there is a payoff or penalty. It takes focus and concentration to listen when we are disinterested or we hear something that is of no value to us at the moment. When your mind wanders, you can get back to listening by taking some or all of the following actions:

✖ Forget your own agenda for a few moments.

✖ Invite random thoughts to leave as graciously as they entered and re-focus on the speaker.

✖ Remember the importance of the speaker and mentally review and process his or her words.

✖ Search for non-verbal clues such as facial expressions, posture, gestures, and vocal tone to help you decode messages and understand the speaker's meaning.

✖ Make eye contact and show that you are listening and that you care.

✖ Listen for positive intentions and for the possibilities that the speaker is communicating.

✖ Find areas of common interest and agreement.

There are many benefits to be gained by learning how to give someone your undivided attention. It will create an ease and grace in your manner that the speaker will sense, be grateful for, and respond to. And, if you pay attention, you will be able to observe non-verbal messages that often reveal more than the words.

Remember What is Being Said

Listening occurs in the moment. You have about two seconds after hearing something to decide whether or not you will retain it.

If you want to win friends and influence people, remember their names. It is the supreme compliment and is a learned skill. For years I convinced myself I was not able to remember names. That was another bit of self-delusion. The following techniques have helped me improve my ability to remember names.

- ✘ Stop and give undivided attention to someone for a few seconds when you first hear his or her name.

- ✘ Try not to think about yourself when being introduced.

- ✘ Repeat the name immediately after you have heard it.

- ✘ Study the person's face and physical appearance as you say his or her name to yourself.

- ✘ Review the name again as soon as the person has left.

- ✘ Link the name with a feature of the person, e.g., Barry is hairy or Paul is tall.

Exercise

Rebecca Shafir suggests in *The Zen of Listening* that you purposely turn the volume on the TV down when you want to turn it up. Let the dog bark and let the dishwasher whirl in the background. Put all of your attention on what the person on TV is communicating. This exercise will help you concentrate in noisy situations that are not under your control.

PART IV

Step 4:
Don't Interrupt or Offer Unsolicited Advice and Solutions

Wise men talk because they have something to say; fools because they have to say something.

—Plato

Management consultant Erline Stitcher said, *The first person to take a breath is considered the designated listener.* I have this insatiable desire to interrupt, get to the point, and fix things for other people. I am much better off when I concentrate on my own life lessons instead of trying to teach others theirs. If you can stop interrupting and giving unsolicited advice or solutions, you will score big points with everyone.

Interrupting

The more you talk, the less you listen. The more you talk, the less others will listen. I love to interrupt and get to the point; women hate it when I interrupt. If you want to get along and be appreciated by the woman in your life and others, bite your tongue and stop interrupting!

Unsolicited Advice and Solutions

Our culture teaches us to speak first, listen second, and observe third. More effective listeners observe first, listen next, and speak last.

It's best to refrain from giving unsolicited advice or solutions to grown-ups. The suggestions are seldom appreciated or acted upon, and no matter how lovingly they are given, they have a negative connotation. The underlying message is that the advice giver is smarter and knows more than the receiver. Most healthy adults are quite capable of making decisions, especially when they are aware of the options.

Life is a complicated dance. Advice you gave in good faith may not apply if the music changes. My personal goal is to take at least ten percent of the advice I have already given to others.

If your opinion is asked, trust the speaker's instincts and ability to find his or her solutions. Suggest alternatives like

✘ Have you thought of other options?

✘ How do you feel about alternatives?

✘ What do you plan to do about it?

If the speaker insists on hearing your advice, opinion, or solutions keep them short and make it clear that the comments are made from your point of view.

PART IV

Step 5:
Give Feedback to Show You're Listening

The Path of More Effective Listening

Oscar Wilde wrote, *He knew the precise psychological moment when to say nothing.*

Since the speaker cannot read your mind, it is important that you are perceived as listening. More effective listeners can be best described as quiet, attentive, interested, comfortable, alert, poised, patient, focused, selfless, generous, thoughtful, involved, curious, caring, loving, accepting, and understanding. If you can't be all of the above, try a few at a time.

The quality of your listening is judged by the nature of your responses and questions and whether the speaker feels that he or she has been heard. Giving non-verbal feedback is a great way to let the speaker know you are interested in what is being said. These non-verbal clues work well.

✘ Smile, nod frequently, and have a positive look on your face.

✘ Turn your body toward the speaker in a direct face-to-face orientation.

✘ Sit up in a relaxed position and lean forward slightly. It is difficult to look enthusiastic while slouching.

✘ Keep arms to your side, hands not touching, and legs uncrossed.

Sylvester Stallone said in *Rocky, Ya know, I ain't use to talking to a closed door.*

Once the speaker is finished, pause and then act like a sounding board and mirror his or her thoughts and feelings in your own words. To know if you understand the speaker's intention, rephrase and repeat back what you heard and ask if your understanding is correct.

Offer limited, specific feedback that is encouraging to the speaker. It should be descriptive, clear, and objective. Positive feedback is a reflection of feelings and meaning from the listener's point of view.

Door Openers for Feedback

A door opener is an invitation for the speaker to talk. It might take two or three door openers before the speaker realizes that you care and are listening. Some examples of door openers:

- ✖ I appreciate you sharing this with me
- ✖ You are making an important point
- ✖ What brought you to that conclusion?
- ✖ I'm glad you brought that up
- ✖ Please go on, I am interested in what you are saying
- ✖ Mmm hmm
- ✖ I'm listening
- ✖ Oh, I see
- ✖ Right
- ✖ Then?

✘ You bet

✘ And?

✘ Go on, so?

✘ I hear you

✘ Sure

✘ Darn!

✘ Wow!

✘ Thank you for sharing that information

✘ Please continue

Door Closers for Feedback

A door closer is an invitation for the speaker to withdraw. One heavy door closer is all it takes. Some examples of door closers are as follows:

✘ Any question that puts the speaker in a defensive position (the question "why" often elicits a defensive posture...Why did you do that?)

✘ I heard you (without saying what you heard)

✘ I see you're upset (without being specific about what may be upsetting the speaker)

✘ No, it's not true

✘ Tell me why you did that

✘ You made a mistake

✖ You are wrong

✖ Why would you think that?

✖ You are not telling me the truth

✖ The use of certain words:
should/ shouldn't
must
always/never
but (negates what was said previously)
except/however
don't
have to
got to
can't
wouldn't

Ask Questions Only to Clarify

The Dalai Lama says, *Remember that silence is sometimes the best answer.*

In the past, the purpose of me asking a question was to show off my intelligence so the answer was not awfully important. When you ask a question remember that you may be redirecting the speaker's thoughts. Ask yourself, "Is my goal to ask a question or to interrupt and control the conversation?"

✖ Before you ask a question, acknowledge the speaker by paraphrasing his or her words by saying something like "So what you were saying is…"

The Path of More Effective Listening

✗ To get a positive response, ask questions from a position of interest, curiosity, and objectivity. The questions ought to encourage the speaker to expand on what he or she has been communicating.

✗ Make questions brief and to the point.

✗ Take notes and wait to ask questions until the speaker is finished.

✗ Resist luring the speaker into a trap by asking questions you think will prove that he or she is wrong and that you are right.

✗ Ask a question only when you are prepared to hear the answer.

✗ Remember the answers.

✗ Ask open-ended questions that require more than a one- or two-word answer. Some examples of open-ended questions are

  ◆ Why do you feel that way?
  ◆ What do you think?
  ◆ How may I help you?
  ◆ Tell me more about how you feel?
  ◆ Please tell me about your day.
  ◆ Tell me more.
  ◆ Can you elaborate?

✗ Avoid closed-end questions that can be answered with a yes, no, fine, or good. Some examples are

- How was your day?
- Did you have a good time?
- Do you feel okay?
- Did you like what you saw?

Door Openers to Clarify

- ✖ What I understand you to say...
- ✖ What I heard you say was...(not what you said was)
- ✖ Let me try putting this in my own words...
- ✖ What I think you are saying is...
- ✖ I heard you say a few minutes ago...
- ✖ Could you repeat...?
- ✖ Did you say...?
- ✖ Did you mean...?
- ✖ It sounds like...
- ✖ Is that correct? (avoid use of "right")
- ✖ What exactly do you think is wrong?
- ✖ How would you describe your...?
- ✖ Sorry, perhaps I didn't ask the question correctly.
- ✖ Are these the questions you are asking...?
- ✖ I think we both agree that...

Door Closers to Clarify

- ✘ Cutting off, criticizing, or interrupting the speaker.

- ✘ Playing the devil's advocate and pointing out all of the negatives.

- ✘ Attempting to manipulate and gain control by changing the subject or asking too many questions.

- ✘ Being sarcastic.

- ✘ Cross examination that puts the speaker on the defensive and requires an explanation or defense of his or her behavior.

- ✘ Finishing the speaker's thoughts and sentences.

PART IV

Step 6:
Listen with the Goal to Understand, Not with the Intent to Talk

...One person who is truly understanding, who takes the trouble to listen to us as we consider a problem can change our outlook on the whole world.

—Dr. E.H. Mayo

I spent most of my listening time in the past waiting to talk about my own experiences. I made limited eye contact, paid no attention to non-verbal messages, and heard only the gist of a conversation. I was only interested in my perception of what was being said, not in what was being communicated.

There is much more to effective listening than hearing the gist of a conversation. Your whole being, including your heart, needs to be involved in the process. When understanding is your goal, even those who are speaking in anger or with emotional intensity can be understood. You will be able to relate to anyone, even your teenagers!

Listen with Your Whole Being

Lyndon Johnson said, *The most important thing a man has to tell you is what he is not telling you.*

The Path of More Effective Listening

The quality of my life and those around me improved dramatically when I began to rest my tongue and use my ears, brain, eyes, instincts, and heart to understand both verbal *and* non-verbal messages.

Most of an iceberg lies under the water and most of the meaning in communication lies hidden beneath the words. Surveys show communication is

    7%   words (verbal)
  38%   vocal tone and voice cues
  55%   eye contact, body language,
           and facial expressions

Let's see how your ears, eyes, brain, and instincts relate to more effective listening.

Ears

- Accurately receive and transfer sounds to the brain.
- Pay attention to the pitch, pace, articulation, resonance, tone, emphasis, volume, and any other subtleties of the speaker's voice that might communicate feelings and/or meaning.

PART IV

Brain

- Keep an open mind and be flexible enough to modify your position.

- Have no expectations of what you are to accomplish by listening.

- Be accepting and you will help make the speaker feel safe without the fear of ridicule and rejection.

- Listen to the message and the messenger.

Eyes

Yogi Berra wrote, *You can observe a lot by watching.* Why is it when I stare at a woman's body she knows that I am staring even when she is looking in another direction? The answer is that women have eyes everywhere.

- Recognize that the single most important element of listening with your whole being is eye contact. When you look deeply into someone's eyes, you are witnessing their heart and soul.

- Make eye contact most of the time with your eyes wide open, without staring. Notice the color of the person's eyes. Most speakers feel flattered and impressed when a listener is in eye contact. It shows you are interested and ready to receive.

The Path of More Effective Listening

- ◆ Understand that words have different meanings to different people. You can evaluate content, ideas, and feelings by observing the speaker's eyes, body language, expressions, and voice.

When it comes to understanding someone's feelings, his or her face and body language can speak volumes. By merely observing, you can identify emotions like happiness, sadness, surprise, concern, fear, anger, disgust, and bewilderment.

Instincts

Trust the instinct to the end,
though you can render no reason.

—Ralph Waldo Emerson

- ◆ Instincts speak to us in a language that is specific to each one of us. More effective listening gives us direct access to our instincts so that trusting them is then an option.

Door Openers for Whole Being Listening

- ✘ Being interested in what is being said
- ✘ Giving honest compliments
- ✘ Saving the rebuttals

✘ Reinforcing the speaker by giving positive feedback that encourages the conversation to continue

Door Closers for Whole Being Listening

✘ Acting like a forced, pretend, or selective listener

✘ Showing a lack of interest in the speaker's experiences and ideas

✘ Being judgmental or a "know-it-all"

✘ Looking around the room and appearing restless, impatient, bored, or nervous

✘ Analyzing the speaker's faults

✘ Rushing the speaker

✘ Not responding to a speaker's request

✘ Making the speaker feel that you have already made up your mind

✘ Forgetting what was said

✘ Hearing some of the words and paying attention to little else

✘ Displaying negative body language such as folding your arms, looking at your watch, looking away, frowning, or fidgeting

✘ Being so emotionally upset that it interferes with your ability to understand

✘ Playing therapist or interpreter by analyzing the speaker

✘ Giving unsolicited advice, opinions, or offering solutions

✘ Jumping to conclusions before understanding

✘ Being defensive

Exercise

Watch a TV sitcom or drama with the sound turned off. What is the mood of the program and do you have a sense of what is happening? Share your observations with a family member or friend who watched the same show with sound.

Listening with the Heart

Listening is an attitude of the heart,
a genuine desire to be with another
that both attracts and heals.

— J. Isham

A man rubbed a bottle and out came a genie that said, "I lost a fortune in the stock market so I can offer you only one wish." The man's dream was to visit Hawaii but he was afraid to fly or travel on a ship. For his one wish, the man asked the genie to build a bridge from California to Hawaii. The genie said, "That's too hard a of job even for a genie. Do you have another wish?" The man asked to be able to understand what women are feeling and what they really mean. The genie asked, "Do you want two lanes or four?"

Listening with the heart is not about understanding feelings, it is about acknowledging them. If you want to experience a high level of bliss, learn how to listen well enough to acknowledge the feelings of your wife or girlfriend. I know It means breaking the macho guy code: "Do not under any circumstances, except maybe funerals, deal with feelings or talk about them honestly."

Being emotionally authentic by processing and sharing feelings is not an easy job for most of us mortal men. We usually become successful in our careers by repressing our vulnerability and feelings, not by expressing them. And most of us either don't understand or don't want to understand our feelings because there is no clear evidence that this awareness will make us any happier.

On the other hand, listening and acknowledging your wife or girlfriend's feelings will bring you much happiness and it is easier to do than you think.

In *The Lost Art of Listening*, Michael Nichols writes, *You don't have to be responsible for someone's feelings to be aware of them and to acknowledge them.* Webster defines "acknowledge" as "...to take notice...to recognize...to be aware of." You can acknowledge your partner's feelings without agreeing, sympathizing, or completely understanding them. Nor do you have to change who you are or let feelings manage your life. Keep in mind that feelings are neither right or wrong.

A cab driver once told me, "Women have to talk so many words a day for so long or they just don't feel right." Talking about feelings is the fundamental way women create intimacy and friendships. And remember that when a woman asks you to share your feelings, she is often asking you to be in touch with hers.

To become aware of your partner's feelings, make eye contact, listen for vocal tones, and observe her body language. Most feelings fall into one or more of four categories: sad, angry, scared, and happy. To help me remember, I think of SASH. It is no accident that "happy" is last. Women don't seem to have the same need to process happy feelings as they do the other three.

When your partner is finished talking and processing, instead of telling her what to do, be interested in what was communicated and make an educated guess as to which SASH she might have been feeling. Say something like, "It sounds like you're (pick one or more) sad, angry, scared, or happy." Unless you guessed happy when she was not, expect shocked and delighted looks that will translate into a high level of bliss in your home.

If you want to expand your description of feelings and make more points with the women in your life, consult the Feelings Dictionary in the Appendix of this book.

To reach an even higher level of bliss, listen well enough to be able to acknowledge the feelings of the rest of your family (especially teenagers) and the challenging people at work. To get to this level takes more work because few of us would consider asking a wife or girlfriend to help guide us through the process.

The highest level of bliss is when you listen well enough to be aware of your own feelings and have the courage to openly and honestly share them with your partner. The few saint-like men who reach this level of bliss earn the equivalent of an M.L.A. graduate listening degree (Master of Love and Affection) with all of its attendant benefits.

Door Openers for Feelings

- ✗ You look happy, do you want to share it with me?
- ✗ Something seems to be bothering you. Care to talk about it?
- ✗ That must have been upsetting.
- ✗ Do you feel hurt by that?
- ✗ It sounds like you feel strongly about that.
- ✗ How does that make you feel?
- ✗ I respect your right to feel that way.
- ✗ What are your concerns?
- ✗ I care about you and am available to listen.
- ✗ So your concern is...
- ✗ From your point of view...
- ✗ It sounds like something you need to handle. I'll support you however I can.
- ✗ Do I have a correct understanding of how you feel?
- ✗ Where did you last have your car keys?

Door Closers for Feelings

- ✗ I understand what you are saying (you are dismissing and discounting their feelings rather than acknowledging what they are).

- ✗ I don't agree with your feelings.

- ✗ How can anyone who is as smart as you are feel that way?

- ✗ You don't honestly feel that way, do you?

- ✗ You don't need to feel that way.

- ✗ You are making too much of a fuss about this.

- ✗ What a sourpuss you have on today.

- ✗ Don't inflict your lousy mood on me.

- ✗ Don't mope around all day, that won't help anything.

- ✗ I'm sure whatever happened wasn't worth ruining your day over.

- ✗ Cheer up. Things will get better, they always do.

- ✗ It will blow over. Next week you won't even remember what you felt.

- ✗ It's not that bad.

- ✗ You're hypersensitive.

- ✗ If you feel that way then it's hopeless.

- ✗ Why are you always losing your damn keys?

The Path of More Effective Listening

Exercise

Your choice and use of feeling words is important. To practice your ability to recognize feelings, write one or more of the four SASH choices (sad, angry, scared, or happy) next to each statement.

Hey, you won't believe this! I just got a compliment from my sister.

Feeling_____

Don't touch that. It's mine!

Feeling_____

Why don't you tell me what's bothering you? You never say anything when I ask you about it.

Feeling_____

Just when I thought everything was going well, my mother tells me I'm still not doing things right. What does she expect?

Feeling_____

First thing this morning the hot water tank burst, the kids were fighting, and I had a migraine headache. I just wanted to go back to bed.

Feeling_____

I just found out I have cancer and don't know if I should tell the children

Feeling_____

The rumor is that my company is being bought out and I may lose my job

Feeling_____

PART IV

Anger and Emotional Intensity

A survey conducted by Shere Hite found that when 4,500 women were asked "What does your partner do that makes you the maddest?", seventy-seven percent responded, "He doesn't listen."

Before allowing someone to make you angry, walk a mile in their shoes. That way you will be a mile away and have their shoes. When feelings of not being understood come out as anger, listening is the key to calming down. Ignoring the angry feeling or fighting back will produce the opposite result.

The way I deal with emotional intensity is by listening and becoming aware of my role in allowing the intensity to remain. I then have the option to decide if I want to do something about it.

I thought I was a half hour early for a family Bar Mitzvah and it turned out that I was a half hour late. Twenty-five family members did not appear happy while standing in a row waiting for me to show up to take a family picture. The hostess, my daughter Julie, asked in a cold, calm voice, "Where were you?"

It was a simple enough question. My immediate reaction was to answer, "It wasn't my fault, no one told me to be here early." I used my newly found listening skills to assess the situation. The tone of my daughter's voice and her body language suggested that I was in big trouble. Her eyes were half closed. Her hands were on her hips with her front leg bent forward in an attack position. I thought I saw steam coming from the top of her head.

After assessing my daughter's non-verbal messages and listening to my own role in what had happened, I decided I would rather be happy than right. I responded, "I did not hear that I was supposed to be here early." My listening skills and choice of words got me only a dirty look and the emotional intensity disappeared.

If someone can push your emotional hot buttons, he or she has control over you. If you cannot contain your anger or frustration, ask for a time out and agree upon another time to listen.

Telling an angry person to calm down is denying his or her right to be upset. If you can handle it, let the speaker vent.

E. F. Benson is quoted as saying, *If people would only hold their tongues on unpleasant topics, how the things themselves would improve.* Some suggestions are offered to help reduce emotional intensity and diffuse the power of words you may not want to hear.

- Think about the speaker's best intention
- Maintain eye contact
- Let the speaker continue
- Be silent and attentive
- Breathe deeply and slowly

- Keep your voice soft and steady
- Pause and wait before speaking
- Do not plan a response
- Agree with what you can
- Apologize if you mean it
- Help the speaker feel understood, not put down.
- Propose that you each be allowed to present your point of view only after restating the ideas and feelings of the other person to their satisfaction.

Exercise

Pair up with someone. One of you will be the speaker and the other the listener. The speaker is to talk about an important topic that he or she is angry and/or frustrated about.

For sixty seconds the listener is to act like he or she is not listening. For another sixty seconds the listener will become a more effective listener. Use some of the door openers and closers listed throughout this book.

When done, discuss the experience with your partner. What was it like to not be listened to, and what was it like to be listened to? What did it feel like when you were speaking and sensed negative or positive physical and emotional responses from the listener?

Reverse roles. For sixty seconds the speaker becomes the listener and the listener becomes the speaker. After about a minute discuss the experience.

Listening to teenagers

I am not young enough to know everything.

—Sir James M. Barrie

The average family with teenagers spends only about fourteen minutes a day engaging in parent/child face-to- face communication. Twelve of those minutes are taken up with such topics as what's for dinner? who needs a ride? and where is the remote?

If you want to communicate more effectively with teenagers, spend more quality listening time with them. And remember these words of wisdom from Robert Fulghum, *Don't worry that children never listen to you; worry that they are always watching you.*

Give your teen a Gold Listening Card to use on a regular basis and try some of the following strategies.

✘ Be available to listen when a teen wants to talk.

✘ Listen while you share an activity your teenager might enjoy, like driving or taking a walk.

✖ Respect the fact that like adults, teens have moods.

✖ Remember it is not productive to attempt to force a teenager to talk or listen. Not responding may be a teen's way of exerting individual power.

✖ Keep communication channels open by encouraging your teenager's attempts to share sensitive and negative information or feelings.

✖ Follow Kimberly Keith's advice and "don't feel that you must advise or help your child come up with a solution all the time. The value of listening is in the listening itself."

✖ Show patience when a teenager is struggling to explain something. Limit your questions and choose your words carefully. Ask short and simple open-ended questions to show your interest and involvement. If a teen thinks you are prying or interrogating, he or she will shut down immediately.

✖ Be creative and paraphrase your responses. Teenagers usually object when their exact words are repeated back to them.

✖ Talk about and acknowledge a teen's needs and feelings. Separate the person from the deed.

- ✘ Let a teenager know that his or her thoughts and ideas are valued, that they are loved and appreciated and are unique, special people.

- ✘ Brainstorm together to find mutually agreeable solutions. Avoid giving advice and making evaluations unnecessarily. Try to determine whether or not the teenager realizes why a particular action is acceptable or unacceptable, wise or unwise. And whether he or she sees the consequences of the behavior.

- ✘ Suspend judgment until you hear the the whole story.

Carl Jung wrote, *If there is anything we wish to change in the child, we should first examine it and see whether it is not something that could better be changed in ourselves.*

Door Openers for Teenagers

- ✘ I love and believe in you.
- ✘ Could it be that...?
- ✘ Correct me if I am wrong.
- ✘ Is it possible that...?
- ✘ It appears that you...
- ✘ I get the impression that...
- ✘ I hear you saying...

✘ From your point of view...

✘ You're feeling...because...

✘ So you're suggesting...

✘ So you figure that...

✘ Just because we argue doesn't mean we don't agree.

Door Closers for Teenagers

✘ Children should be seen and not heard.

✘ Don't argue with me.

✘ You don't know what you are talking about.

✘ Don't interrupt your elders.

✘ Don't be forward.

✘ I am suspicious of you.

✘ Shut up and listen.

✘ You are too young to understand.

✘ Don't speak until you are spoken to.

✘ Look at me when I am talking to you.

✘ We don't listen to those things in our family.

✘ Don't pay any attention to him/her.

✘ Pretend you didn't notice.

✘ Don't take it so seriously.

Exercise

Have dinnertime family discussions where a topic is assigned and everyone comes prepared to talk about it. Adults are to slow down on the parenting and become equal participants. Pull numbers out of a hat to determine the order of speaking and set the same time limit for each speaker. There are to be no interruptions. The next person can give his or her views only after paraphrasing the thoughts, ideas, and feelings of the previous speaker to the previous person's satisfaction.

Some of the topics can be controversial and some are safe. The following examples are good topics for this exercise.

- A wedding party and a funeral meet at a crossroad. Who has the right of way?
- The way to combat terrorism is...
- I think our government...
- The drinking age...
- Capital punishment is...
- When I relate to people I...
- I'm at my best when...
- Those who don't know me well...
- An important family value to me is...
- My family...
- I enjoy people who...

- ◆ One important thing I have learned this year is...
- ◆ One of my biggest regrets is...
- ◆ Too many people...
- ◆ I'm really proud of the fact that...

Step 7:
Make an Honest Effort to Understand

Both of my ex-wives said that I did not listen. At least that's what I think they said.

Being able to understand and then see the big picture is not always easy. The government created the Federal Air Transportation Airline Security Service for our protection. When coming up with a name for an agency which has a serious purpose, did the Washington bureaucrats take the time to understand how air travelers might feel about our safety when we see highly trained men and women in their black jackets with the initials F.A.T.A.S.S. displayed on their backs?

You don't have to completely understand another person. You will make a lot of points by listening and *trying* to understand those near and dear to you.

If you listen with the goal of understanding others, you are not only gaining knowledge that will help you make intelligent, caring, and loving responses, you are taking advantage of the law of cause and effect. You will attract people who will listen with the goal of understanding you.

Imagine how much closer we might be to harmony and peace in the Middle East if moderate Israelis and Palestinians met face-to-face with everyone making a real effort to understand each other's points of view, needs, and feelings.

You will achieve an even higher level of bliss if you learn how to listen and understand yourself. By listening and becoming aware of my role in allowing stress to remain in my life, I then have the option to take action to remove it.

Let's review the steps along the path of more effective listening.

- ✘ Step 1: Have the Desire, Make a commitment
- ✘ Step 2: Accept the Challenges and Recognize the Opportunities
- ✘ Step 3: Pay Attention
- ✘ Step 4: Don't Interrupt or Offer Unsolicited Advice and Solutions
- ✘ Step 5: Give Feedback to Show You're Listening
- ✘ Step 6: Listen with the Goal to Understand, Not with the Intent to Talk.
- ✘ Step 7: Make an Honest Effort to Understand

PART IV

As you pass out your **Gold Listening Cards** and practice more effective listening each day, remember that it is not always easy for another person to say what he or she means in a clear easy-to-understand language. Instead of blaming the speaker for a lack of clarity, *assume ninety percent of the responsibility for listening and understanding* what is being communicated. If you don't understand, don't be shy about admitting it.

Calvin Coolidge has been credited with saying, *No one ever listened themselves out of a job or marriage*. To help improve your understanding of another person:

✘ Pause when the speaker is finished and don't be uncomfortable with the silence. While hesitating, maintain eye contact and think about the speaker's point of view, feelings, and supporting reasons. Come from a place of "it's not right or wrong" and remember that it is the speaker's opinion.

✘ Before responding, judging, forming an opinion, or making a decision, take the time to ask yourself if you understand what the speaker meant and what he or she needs from you. And when appropriate, ask yourself before responding whether you want to be right or happy.

The Path of More Effective Listening

✖ Be aware that you can understand the speaker without agreeing because listening and agreeing are separate acts.

✖ Paraphrase the speaker's thoughts and feelings in your own words and then ask the speaker to acknowledge that you understand.

You will know that you have become a more effective listener when, in addition to receiving the benefits, the woman in your life says, "You are a good listener for a guy." That's about as good as it gets for us.

When you've learned how to listen;
well, that's when you've learned
everything you need to know in life.

—Glynn David Harris
1999 International Listening
Association Listener of the year

PART IV

Remembering the Journey

Please use the following pages to record some of your thoughts on your journey to becoming a more effective listener.

I thought becoming a more effective listener would be

_____

_____

and I was_____

_____.

I thought it would be simple to_____

_____

_____.

I learned it was difficult for me to_____

_____

_____.

The first time I recognized I was making progress in becoming a more effective listener was when _____

_____

_____.

It made me feel_____

_____

_____.

The Path of More Effective Listening

At work, when I listen, I know I still need to ____

_____

_____.

If I do, I expect the benefits will be _____

_____

_____.

When I'm trying to be a more effective listener
for the woman in my life, I know I need to _____

_____

_____.

If I do this, it will benefit our relationship
because _____

_____

_____.

To become a more effective listener for my
family I still need to _____

_____

_____.

If I do, I think my family will feel_____

_____

_____.

For me, the three biggest advantages of
becoming a more effective listener are _____

_____

_____.

Postscript

I would appreciate hearing from you as to how this book may have affected your life along with any listening experiences you are willing to share. And, since listening is a continuous process, I welcome any suggestions you might have as to how this book might be improved in future editions. I am also interested in hearing from anyone who is willing to help introduce the subject of listening to our public school systems.

You can reach me
by clicking "Contact Us" on our website
http://www.WeDoListen.com

If you would like to order a copy of this book for a friend, it is available through your local bookstore, Amazon.com or our website,
WeDoListen.com.

*It is the province of knowledge to speak.
And it is the privilege of wisdom to listen.*

—Oliver Wendell Holmes

Feelings Dictionary

Feelings of Anger

Aggravated	Enraged	Outraged
Angry	Furious	Peeved
Annoyed	Hateful	Perturbed
Belligerent	Hostile	Resentful
Bugged	Infuriated	Seething
Bitter	Irked	Spiteful
Cruel	Irritated	Vengeful
Disgusted	Mad	Vindictive
Disturbed	Mean	Violent

Feelings of Sadness

Abandoned	Down	Neglected
Alienated	Empty	Resigned
Alone	Estranged	Rejected
Anguished	Forlorn	Sad
Ashamed	Forsaken	Sorrowful
Awful	Grief-stricken	Thwarted
Blue	Humiliated	Unhappy
Crushed	Hurt	Unloved
Defeated	Isolated	Weepy
Depressed	Lonely	Worried
Desolate	Low	
Despair	Melancholy	
Despondent	Miserable	
Devastated	Misunderstood	

PART IV

Feelings of Fear

Afraid	Frightened	Tense
Alarmed	Horrified	Terrified
Anxious	Intimidated	Threatened
Apprehensive	Nervous	Trapped
Desperate	Panicky	Uneasy
Fearful	Persecuted	Unsafe
Frantic	Scared	Worried

Feelings of Inadequacy

Bewildered	Helpless	Psychotic
Broken	Ignored	Put upon
Confused	Impotent	Rejected
Cheated	Inadequate	Shameful
Condemned	Incapable	Shy
Cowardly	Ineffective	Small
Crippled	Inferior	Stupid
Deficient	Insecure	Timid
Demoralized	Insignificant	Unable
Disabled	Isolated	Unappreciated
Dominated	Insufficient	Unheard
Done for	Intimidated	Useless
Empty	Left out	Unwanted
Enervated	Lonely	Vulnerable
Exasperated	Muddled	Washed up
Feeble	Out of touch	Weak
Foolish	Paralyzed	Worthless
Frantic	Pitiful	
Guilty	Powerless	

Feelings Dictionary

Feelings of Stress

Ambivalent	Disturbed	Repressed
Anxious	Doubtful	Shocked
Astonished	Dumbfounded	Stunned
Baffled	Embarrassed	Tense
Betrayed	Exasperated	Terrible
Bewildered	Flustered	Tired
Bored	Frustrated	Tormented
Bothered	Horrible	Tortured
Burdened	Hopeless	Trapped
Caught	Hysterical	Troubled
Concerned	Imposed upon	Uncomfortable
Defensive	Irked	Uneasy
Depressed	Jealous	Unsafe
Disjointed	Jumpy	Unsettled
Dissatisfied	Overwhelmed	Unsure
Distant	Pained	Upset
Distraught	Perplexed	Vulnerable
Distressed	Pressured	

Feelings of Happiness

Aglow	Fantastic	Overjoyed
Blissful	Fulfilled	Pleased
Calm	Gay	Proud
Charmed	Glad	Relaxed
Cheerful	Good	Relieved
Content	Great	Satisfied
Eager	Happy	Surprised
Ecstatic	High	Thrilled

Elated	Included	Understood
Enthused	Joyous	Wonderful
Excited	Jubilant	

Feelings of Love and Caring

Adorable	Cooperative	Loving
Affable	Devoted	Peaceful
Affectionate	Empathic	Safe
Altruistic	Forgiving	Sensitive
Amiable	Friendly	Sympathetic
Caring	Genuine	Tender
Cherished	Helpful	Wanted
Close	Humane	Warm
Compassionate	Intimate	Whole
Concerned	Kind	
Considerate	Loveable	

Feelings of Adequacy

Able	Effective	Powerful
Adequate	Energetic	Robust
Bold	Fearless	Secure
Brave	Forceful	Self-assured
Capable	Healthy	Stable
Competent	Important	Strong
Confident	Mighty	Worthy
Dynamic	Nervy	
Eager	Okay	

Feelings Dictionary

Add your own "feeling" words

Further Reading and Listening

Adler, M. *How to Speak, How to Listen*. New York: Simon & Schuster, 1997.

Barker, L. and K. Watson. *Listen Up, How to Improve Relationships, Reduce Stress, and Be More Productive by Using the Power of Listening.* New York: St. Martins Press, 2000.

Bohm, D. *On Dialogue*. New York: Routledge, 1996.

Bolton, R. *People Skills: How to Assert Yourself, Listen to Others and Resolve Conflicts.* New York: Simon and Schuster, 1996.

Bone, D. *The Business of Listening*. National Book Network, 1988.

Brownell, J. *Listening, Attitudes, Principles, and Skills*. Boston: Allyn and Bacon, 1996.

Burley-Allen, M. *Listening, the Forgotten Skill: A Self-Teaching Guide*, 2nd ed. New York: John Wiley & Sons, Inc., 1995.

Further Reading and Listening

Condrill, J. and B. Bough. *101 Ways to Improve Your Communication Skills Instantly*. Virginia: GoalMinds, 1998.

Covey, Stephen R. *The 7 Habits of Highly Effective People*. New York: Simon and Schuster, 1990.

Covey, Stephen R. *The 7 Habits of Highly Effective People*, audiotape: order #72026.

Devereaux, R. *Power Listening, Easy to Use Tools for Improved Communication*, audiotape, 1997.

Faber, A. and E. Mazlish. *How to Talk So Kids Will Listen & Listen So Kids Will Talk*. New York: Avon Books, 1980.

Farrell, W. *Women Can't Hear What Men Don't Say: Destroying Myths, Creating Love*. New York: Penguin Putnam, Inc., 2000.

Fisher, R. and W. Ury. *Getting to Yes, Negotiating Agreement without Giving In.*, New York: Penguin Books, 1981.

John Gray, Ph.D. *Men Are From Mars, Women Are From Venus.*, New York: HarperCollins, 1992.

Halley, R. *How Audiences Listen: Critical Information for the Public Speaker*. Missouri: Kaia Publishing, 1999.

Kratz, D. and A.R. Kratz, *Effective Listening Skills*. Mirror Press, 1995.

Madaule, P. *When Listening Comes Alive: A Guide to Effective Learning and Communication*. Ontario, Canada: Moulin Publishing, 1994.

Miller, S., P. Miller, E. Nunnally, and D. Wackman, *Talking and Listening Together. Colorado: Interpersonal Communications, Inc., 1991.*

Nichols, M. *The Lost Art of Listening, How Learning To Listen Can Improve Relationships*. New York: The Guilford Press.

Rogers, C. *A Way Of Being*. New York: Houghton Mifflin Company, 1980.

Schmidt, W. and B.J.G. Hateley. *Is It Always Right to Be Right?* New York: AMACOM, 2001.

Further Reading and Listening

Shafir, R. *The Zen Of Listening, Mindful Communication In The Age Of Distraction*. Wheaton, Illinois: The Theosophical Publishing House, 2000.

Shapiro, S. *Listening for Success, How to Master the Most Important Skill of Network Marketing*. California: Chica Publications, 1999.

Tannen, D. *That's Not What I Meant!: How Conversational Style Makes Or Breaks Relationships*. New York: William Morrow and Company, 1986.

Tannen, D. *You Just Don't Understand: Women and Men In Conversation*. New York: Ballantine Books, 1980.

Tannen, D. *I Only Say This Because I Love You: How The Way We Talk Can Make or Break Family Relationships Throughout Our Lives*. New York: Random House, 2001.

Trujillo, M. *Why Can't We Talk? What Teens Would Share If Parents Would Listen*. Florida: Health Communications, Inc., 2000.

Van Nagel, C. E.J. Reese, M. Reese, and R. Siudzinski Mega. *Teaching and Learning*. Oregon: Metamorphous Press, 1985.

Watson, K. and L. Barker. *Winning by Listening Around: 21 Keys To Smarter Listening*. Louisiana: SPECTRA, Inc., 1995.

Wolff, F. and N. Marsnik. *Perceptive Listening*, 2nd ed. Texas: Harcourt Brace Jovanovich College Publishers, 1983.

Wolvin, A. and C.G. Coakley. *Listening*, 5th ed. Massachusetts: McGraw-Hill Publishing, 1996.

About the Author

Howard Binkow graduated from the University of Michigan with a bachelor's degree in communications and has had successful careers in home building, radio, sales, sales training, and being a bum.

The author is passionate about more effective listening because it has led him to having everything he needs in life including more than enough money, better relationships, and other goodies.

Howard Binkow became a millionaire homebuilder and then spent several years having a ball spending all the money he made. At age sixty, after discovering the secrets of more effective listening and with no previous experience in sales, he launched a wildly successful career as a salesman. Today, he works ten hours a week and values his work time at $1,000 per hour.

The author's first book, *What It Means to Be A Man*, is on hold to allow further research on the topic.

Gold Listening Card

This card entitles bearer to 15 minutes of my face-to-face undivided attention. I commit to listen with the goal to understand what is being communicated, not with the intent to talk. I agree to acknowledge feelings and promise not to interrupt or offer unsolicited advice and solutions. I will listen in the same way, as I would have others listen to me.

Signed_____

WeDoListen.com

Gold Listening Card

This card entitles bearer to 15 minutes of my face-to-face undivided attention. I commit to listen with the goal to understand what is being communicated, not with the intent to talk. I agree to acknowledge feelings and promise not to interrupt or offer unsolicited advice and solutions. I will listen in the same way, as I would have others listen to me.

Signed_____

WeDoListen.com

Gold Listening Card

This card entitles bearer to 15 minutes of my face-to-face undivided attention. I commit to listen with the goal to understand what is being communicated, not with the intent to talk. I agree to acknowledge feelings and promise not to interrupt or offer unsolicited advice and solutions. I will listen in the same way, as I would have others listen to me.

Signed_____

WeDoListen.com

Gold Listening Card

This card entitles bearer to 15 minutes of my face-to-face undivided attention. I commit to listen with the goal to understand what is being communicated, not with the intent to talk. I agree to acknowledge feelings and promise not to interrupt or offer unsolicited advice and solutions. I will listen in the same way, as I would have others listen to me.

Signed_____

WeDoListen.com